NATIVE AMERICAN NATIONS

Choctaw

F.A. BIRD

Checkerboard Library

An Imprint of Abdo Publishing
abdobooks.com

ABDOBOOKS.COM

Published by Abdo Publishing, a division of ABDO, PO Box 398166, Minneapolis, Minnesota 55439.

Checkerboard Library™ is a trademark and logo of Abdo Publishing.

Printed in the United States of America, North Mankato, Minnesota
102024
012025

THIS BOOK CONTAINS RECYCLED MATERIALS

Editor: Lauri Nelson
Design: Mighty Media, Inc.

Cover Photograph: Albuquerque Journal/AP Photo
Interior Photographs: Ad_hominem/Shutterstock Images, p. 7; Angel Wynn/NativeStock, pp. 11, 21, 25; Archive Photos/Getty Images, p. 9; Heritage Art/Heritage Images/Getty Images, p. 23; Jesse Grant/Getty Images for Disney, p. 29; John Brueske/Shutterstock Images, p. 5; MPI/Getty Images, p. 27; New Orleans Museum of Art/Wikimedia Commons, p. 13; The Gleaner, Darrin Phegley/AP Photo, p. 19; Universal History Archive/Contributor/Getty Images, p. 17; Visual Studies Workshop/Getty Images, p. 15

Library of Congress Control Number: 2024938796

Publisher's Cataloging-in-Publication Data
Names: Bird, F.A., author.
Title: Choctaw / by F.A. Bird
Description: Minneapolis, Minnesota : ABDO Publishing, 2025 | Series: Native American nations | Includes online resources and index.
Identifiers: ISBN 9781098296209 (lib. bdg.) | ISBN 9798384917311 (ebook)
Subjects: LCSH: Choctaw Indians--Juvenile literature. | Native Americans--Juvenile literature. | Indians of North America--Juvenile literature. | Indigenous peoples--Social life and customs--Juvenile literature. | Cultural anthropology--Juvenile literature.
Classification: DDC 973.0497--dc23

Contents

CHAPTER 1

Homelands

The Choctaw (CHAHK-taw) dialect is from the Muskogean language family. When President Andrew Jackson spoke with the Choctaw, he imitated the phrase *hoka hay*. This Choctaw expression was used to communicate agreement. Eventually, the phrase became the word "okay."

Choctaw homelands were located in the Southeast. Choctaw territory once included parts of present-day Alabama, Mississippi, and Louisiana. Various features were found on Choctaw homelands. Some areas were covered with hilly grasslands. Other parts were filled with forests of oak, hickory, and pine trees. Bald cypress trees and sweet gum trees grew in the swamplands. And, Spanish moss often hung from the trees.

Many animals lived on Choctaw territory. Alligators and turtles roamed along the rivers and in the swamplands. Frogs and snakes also made their homes in these areas.

The Mississippi River formed the western boundary of the Choctaw homelands.

CHAPTER 2

Society

Choctaw society was split into two *iksas*, or parts. Children belonged to their mother's *iksa*. A person was forbidden to marry someone in his or her own *iksa*.

The Choctaw lived in villages. Each village had a chief to represent and protect the people. Chiefs met with a council of elders to discuss the needs of the village. And, they conducted ceremonies. Each chief had an assistant to help organize festivals and announce messages.

District chiefs were another group of Choctaw leaders. They were responsible for a particular area of villages. District chiefs met individually with the village chiefs in their area to discuss issues. When a very important matter arose, all of the district chiefs met with all of the village chiefs. Together, they came to a conclusion.

Each village also had a war chief. These leaders trained young warriors to protect the villages. Each war chief had two assistants to help carry out his orders.

THE CHOCTAW HOMELANDS

CHAPTER 3

Homes

The Choctaw lived in rectangular-shaped homes with triangular roofs. They built using materials found in nature. To make the frame, the Choctaw first buried wooden poles in the ground. Then, they tied crossbeams to the poles using rope made from bark or plant fibers. To form the walls, they wove branches and vines into the frame. Then, they tied woven mats onto the walls.

Finally, the Choctaw covered the outside of the home with **daub**. This protected the interior from harsh weather. They left an opening on one side for a door. And, they left a hole in each end of the roof for smoke to escape.

Inside the homes, there were beds made from branches. The Choctaw covered the beds with woven mats, hides, or fur robes. They made another kind of blanket from turkey feathers. First, they twisted the feathers and rolled them into a string. Then, they wove the string to make a blanket.

Choctaw home covered with large palm leaves

CHAPTER 4

Food

The Choctaw gathered, hunted, and fished. They were also advanced gardeners. The men prepared the land, then the women planted and tended the gardens.

Corn was an important crop for the Choctaw. It was the foundation for many recipes. The Choctaw planted squash, melons, pumpkins, beans, and sunflowers as well.

The women gathered wild fruits, vegetables, nuts, herbs, tree bark, roots, and wild plants. They used these to add flavor to food and to make medicine and drinks.

The men hunted deer, bear, turkeys, rabbits, and ducks with bows and arrows. To catch smaller animals, they used traps, blowguns, and rabbit sticks.

Fishing was common among Choctaw men. They often caught trout and shrimp. Sometimes, they captured alligators. Choctaw men fished with bows and arrows, spears, nets, and hooks and lines. Fish and other meats were dried in the sun or smoked over a fire for later use.

Corn can be made into cornbread. It is cooked inside cornhusks.

CHAPTER 5

Clothing

The Choctaw wore clothing made from deer hides. The women had this job. First, they scraped the meat and hairs from the hides. Then, they **tanned** the hides to make them soft. Next, the women dried the hides and sewed them together. They used needles and **awls** carved from bone and thread made from deer **sinew** or plant fibers.

The women wore dresses. They wore decorated combs in their hair. The men wore **breechcloths**, shirts, and woven sashes. The sashes were hung over the shoulder and tied at the waist. Both men and women wore moccasins with a single front seam with ankle flaps.

Choctaw clothing styles changed after they began trading with the Europeans. The Choctaw traded animal hides and furs for cloth, beads, ribbons, and silver. They used the silver to make combs, armbands, and necklaces. Choctaw men began wearing black felt hats. And, women started decorating their clothing with ribbons.

Sometimes Choctaw women draped a long piece of buckskin over their upper body that wrapped around the left shoulder and tied under the right arm.

CHAPTER 6

Crafts

Choctaw women often wove baskets. They used cane to weave the baskets and vegetable dyes to color them. The women used cane to weave mats for sitting or sleeping on. Sometimes, they hung them on the wall for decoration.

Choctaw men built the equipment that was needed for games, such as stickball. They carved stickball rackets from hickory wood. The rackets were about 30 inches (76 cm) long. The men carved one end to form a loop. Then, they wove the looped end with **sinew** to make a net.

The men also made their hunting tools. They carved rabbit sticks from wood. These were about 18 inches (46 cm) long and shaped like a boomerang. One end had a handle, and the other end was curved. Men used rabbit sticks to kill small animals.

To fish, men used hooks made from bone. To make these, they cut hollow bird bones into sections. Then, they carved the bones into hooks.

Weaving baskets in a group allows younger women to learn the craft.

CHAPTER 7

Family

The Choctaw lived with their extended families. Families attended ceremonies and festivals together. The most important religious ceremony for the Choctaw was the Green Corn Festival. This was held during the summer to celebrate the ripening of corn.

To prepare, the Choctaw cleaned their homes and village. They also **fasted** for two days. Near the end of the festival, a high priest lit a fire and led the elders in a dance around it. This represented the start of a new year.

At some festivals, the Choctaw played games. Stickball was a favorite game. Named "la crosse" by the French, it was played between Choctaw villages to establish peace. Spiritual leaders attended stickball games. Their prayers and powers were thought to affect the game's outcome.

The object of stickball was to use two netted rackets to launch a ball to the opponent's goal. Players used the rackets to pick up, pass, catch, and throw the ball.

Stickball games could involve as few as 20 men and boys, or as many as 300.

CHAPTER 8

Children

A flat forehead on a Choctaw man was a sign of beauty. To obtain this look, the Choctaw used a device that applied pressure to a male infant's forehead. So, the Spanish explorers referred to the tribe as *chato*, which means "flat" in Spanish. Some people believe this is how the Choctaw got their name.

Elders taught Choctaw children about history and **culture** and to respect nature. Children learned to identify plants and animals and to live in harmony with them.

Choctaw women taught girls how to cook food, care for the younger children, prepare hides, and make clothing. Girls made clothing for their dolls. This was good practice for making clothing for their families when they got older.

Choctaw men taught the boys how to make and use blowguns. A full-sized blowgun was up to seven feet (2 m) long, but boys used shorter ones. The boys also learned how to make other tools and weapons.

Nanaiya Robinson shows a bobcat hide to students as part of a Native American cultural presentation. The Robinson family are members of the Choctaw Nation of Oklahoma.

CHAPTER 9

Traditions

The Choctaw share many stories that have been passed on from older generations. The following is a **migration** story. It explains how the Choctaw found their homelands.

Long ago, a group of people lived in the Northwest. The land became too crowded. So two brothers, Chahta and Chicksa, led a migration. They asked the Great Spirit for help and received a special pole. The pole was meant to guide them to their new home in a sacred, plentiful land.

To start, Chahta placed the pole in the ground. The next day it was leaning. So that day, the people traveled in the direction it leaned. This went on for days until they came to a river. Chahta placed the pole in the ground as usual. That night rain poured down. By the next morning, the flooded river had separated the two leaders.

Chicksa continued northward. His group became known as the Chickasaw. Chahta saw the pole standing straight. His group stayed there and became known as the Choctaw.

An original stone marker showing the boundary between their lands has Chock carved on one side and Chick carved on the other.

CHAPTER 10

War

Establishing peace was important to the Choctaw. They often met with neighboring tribes and discussed issues to prevent a war. Leaders sat on woven mats and passed around a peace pipe. This helped to bring balance.

But sometimes, the Choctaw could not establish a peaceful agreement. So, they fought to protect their people and lands. Choctaw women often went into battle with their husbands.

To prepare for war, each village held a dance. A victory during battle was also cause for a lively celebration. The entire village danced, and the warriors shared their stories.

Weapons were mostly the same as hunting tools. The Choctaw used bows and arrows and spears while in battle. During close combat, they used knives and **hatchets**. Early weapons were made of stones, bones, horns, shells, antlers, or wood. Later, the Choctaw began to use guns and metal axes and arrowheads they received in trades.

Chief Moshulatubbee was an excellent Choctaw leader known for his bravery and speaking skills.

CHAPTER II

Contact with Europeans

The Spanish were the first Europeans to meet the Choctaw. Explorer Hernando de Soto arrived in Choctaw territory around 1540. He captured a chief and demanded that the Choctaw carry his group's supplies. The Choctaw were angry, so they made a plan to trick de Soto. At the next village, they held a feast and a dance. When de Soto was off guard, the Choctaw attacked him and his group.

By the early 1700s, the Choctaw had good trade relations with Europeans. At first, there were difficulties because the two groups spoke different languages. So, they developed a special trade language.

The French built trading posts along the Mississippi River. The Choctaw liked to trade with them. The French had valuable goods, such as guns, ribbons, felt hats, and glass beads.

When a Choctaw chief received a peace medal from the US government, he was then called a "great medal chief."

CHAPTER 12

Pushmataha

Pushmataha (push-muh-TAH-hah) was born in Mississippi around 1765. He was a well-known Choctaw warrior, speaker, and negotiator.

In 1805, Pushmataha became a tribal chief. During the Creek War of 1813–1814, he fought against the Creek and British. He also led 500 Choctaw men alongside General Andrew Jackson. For his services, Pushmataha received the rank of brigadier general in the US Army.

Pushmataha embraced the ways of the new settlers more than other Choctaw leaders. He signed treaties that gave parts of Choctaw lands to them. But, he also promoted Native American rights.

In 1824, Pushmataha went to Washington, DC, to strengthen relations between the Choctaw and the federal government. During the trip, he became sick. He died on December 24, 1824. Pushmataha was given a full military funeral and was buried in Washington, DC.

Pushmataha was a respected Choctaw leader.

CHAPTER 13

The Choctaw Today

In 1830, the United States established the Indian Removal Act. This act moved Native American tribes to make room for new settlers. The Choctaw were the first to be relocated. This forced relocation is known as the Trail of Tears. Harsh weather, disease, and lack of food caused the death of about 2,500 Choctaw people on the journey.

The Choctaw Nation of Oklahoma, the Mississippi Band of Choctaw Indians, and the Jena Band of Choctaw Indians are **federally recognized**. All three groups have an elected government. The 2020 Census reported that more than 255,000 people claimed Choctaw ancestry.

The Choctaw work to protect their **culture**. They teach classes to maintain Choctaw language and traditions. The Choctaw Nation of Oklahoma hosts a yearly Labor Day Festival. And, the Mississippi Band of Choctaw Indians hosts an annual Indian Fair. During these celebrations the Choctaw feast, dance, sing, and play stickball.

Chief Gary Batton *(left)* and Assistant Chief Jack Austin Jr. *(right)*. The Choctaw Nation of Oklahoma worked to be sure that Choctaw culture, legends, and history were shown correctly in the TV series "Echo."

Glossary

awl—a pointed tool for marking or making small holes in materials, such as leather or wood.

breechcloth—a piece of hide or cloth, usually worn by men, that is wrapped between the legs and tied with a belt around the waist.

culture—the customs, arts, and tools of a nation or people at a certain time.

daub—a mixture of sand, mud, clay, or crushed seashells used for construction.

dialect—a form of a language spoken in a certain area or by certain people.

extended family—a family that includes grandparents, uncles, aunts, and cousins in addition to a mother, father, and children.

fast—to go without food.

federal recognition—the US government's recognition of a tribe as being an independent nation. The tribe is eligible for special funding and protection of its lands.

hatchet—a short-handled ax often with a hammerhead to be used with one hand.

migrate—to move from one place to another, often to find food.

sinew—a band of tough fibers that joins a muscle to a bone.

tan—to make a hide into leather by soaking it in a special liquid.

ONLINE RESOURCES

Booklinks
NONFICTION NETWORK
FREE! ONLINE NONFICTION RESOURCES

To learn more about the Choctaw, please visit **abdobooklinks.com** or scan this QR code. These links are routinely monitored and updated to provide the most current information available.

Index